Seek the Holy Dark

Clare L. Martin

SEEK THE HOLY DARK
Clare L. Martin

All Poems © Clare L. Martin
© 2017 Yellow Flag Press

Cover art "Birds of Time," digital mixed media
© 2016 by Agnieszka Nowinska
Used with permission

All rights reserved

First Edition
February 2017

ISBN 978-1-365-57723-9

Yellow Flag Press
2275 S. Bascom Ave. #702
Campbell, CA 95008

www.yellowflagpress.com

YFP-137

Praise for *Seek the Holy Dark*

Any new book of poems worth its salt must reinvent the intelligences of poetry: trope, word, image, argument, sentence, strophe, music. The poems in Clare Martin's *Seek the Holy Dark* will keep. They *are* salt.

—Darrell Bourque, Former Louisiana Poet Laureate, author of *Megan's Guitar and Other Poems from Acadie* and *Where I Waited*

Seek the Holy Dark is a book of revelations in poems. Clare L. Martin sees the richness and the poverty that are bedmates, proffers them as gifts, lays them at our feet. Her poems suggest we join in the quest to be both humbled and exalted. Martin, who never looks away, fully understands the duality of nature, its light and darkness, exploring both in this lush and lyrical new collection.

—Susan Tepper, author of *dear Petrov* and *The Merrill Diaries*

From the holy dark of horror storms and freedom in the hand, to starving wolves and old women who live in woods, Clare Martin's poetic imagery seeks in myth to locate depth of soul. She incants salvation "bone by bone" up from the shadows. Her writing has a beautiful fury, a hard questing and secret exultation that keep the reader poised and intoxicated. "Do you seek the heart too" the opening poem asks, and of course, we answer Yes and read breathlessly on. These poems "drop through this world/into dark awakening." The strong-hearted will understand.

—Rachel Dacus, author of *Gods of Water and Air*

Contents

Seek the Holy Dark	8
The Hanging Woman	10
Embellishments	11
In the Marrow all Hunger Begins	12
Dream of Sudden Water	13
The lover who does not come until morning	14
In Mourning	15
Litany	16
Poem to the Madonna	17
Barcelona	18
Aftermath	19
As We Are	20
Woman in Prayer	21
Because We Love	23
Come, a Love Poem	24
Thrice	25
Body in Place	27
Body	28
Barghest	29
For the Electrocuted Owl	30
Stasis	31
Meditation on "Intimations of Winter II"	33
Convergence	34
Ink on a Mirror	35
How It Comes	36
A Rain Like No Other	37
Of the Gone Woman	38
Phoenix	39
What Came After	40
Eiffel Tower, a Recollection of Paris, 1986	41
Refuge	43
Secrets Alluded to but Never Told	44
Seeing Through	45
Sky Burial	46

The Artist and His Model	47
What We Carry	48
The Embalmer's Wife	49
All This Remembering	50
The Hand You Hold	52
The Raw Heart	53
The Word Does Not Come	54
Thunder Found Me	55
When Bones Have Forgotten	56
A Tale	57
A Story	58
Across the Universe	59
End Note	61
Acknowledgments	62
About the Author	63
About the Series	65

Seek the Holy Dark

Seek the Holy Dark

after Jo Ann Tomaselli's "Birds & Fence"

No wind stirs us as we mull
        earth, a sky,
wire-bound wood.
We only surmise the fence
contains a breadth
        for one impenetrable
        moment.
Our pearlescent eyes
sever the heads
of the kings of night,
        when merely perceived.
Bone by bone by bone,
we keep whole
the world's shadow.
And perfume its inhabitants
with an incalculable weather.
You cannot know
        majesty
from mundane: we begat
            all mysteries.
Do you seek the heart, too?
It is made of naked coal,
and the wine which flows
throughout is the remnant
        of horror-storms.
        If we do not fly,
we claw, reap, *hunger*
for that which you leave behind.
We will eat freedom
from your palm
        if you relinquish it.

The Hanging Woman

breathes desert into her throat
Golgotha-naked

rapacious sun
spear opens rib

the most egregious of transgressions
lust inside/out

lungs vigilant flag
serpentine intestine

nailed-out muscles
Heaven's jaw shuts

borne upon the cross
we cannot willfully die

the women tear at their smocks
sun goes

to terminal moonrise
burnt to bone

new meanings of the body impaled;

all sensation thrust
from *pleasured skin*

blade to stone
stone to bone

bone to blood night
incarnated, excarnated.

Embellishments

I am cold in the cathedral. The cold reminds my bones of all the places they have been broken: the metatarsals, the clavicle and the scapulae. I sit on the worn pew. The saints glower. There is a fountain of colored light on marble. Beneath the floor, near the gold altar, a dead bishop is buried. A stone will keep a secret. A gray woman prays on her knees. Her head is a pendulum. She confesses daily, an hour each time, telling sins that she could not possibly commit. What was the name of the old priest who gave Last Rites? He took a pill bottle from the nightstand and slipped it with his rosary into a red felt bag. He left embellishments of forgiveness on the thin skin of my father's brow. A priest has the power to forgive as God forgives, with his very own breath. The day alights on Mary's flesh; illuminates her blue wimple.

In the Marrow all Hunger Begins

carnal wetness
the needle
sensations of wind
a tug at flesh of the low-belly
a harvest
of cerulean veins
hook-eyes
a frazzle of electric wires
coiled   to the womb

an excised heart
as soft palms cup it
transforms
to a tranquilized dove

Beloved jailer,
holy executioner,
Can this sin
be absolved?

I took communion without wine.

Dream of Sudden Water

i
asleep in the woods
dreaming of a fleeting love
the grass sprouts through me

ii
the sky is copper
patinaed with hues of blue
the dream breaks open

iii
a red mare pulls through
apparitions of water
whisperings come

iv
understanding lies
in the soft flicker of sense
in the depth of sleep

v
six crows razed storm clouds
and bled us of all our strength
what madness is this?

vi
a harrowing thought
deep in my petrified bones—
wash me, savior

vii
we drop through this world
into dark awakening
we, the strong-hearted

The lover who does not come until morning
is a leafless tree void of crows,
their unified exodus, and an exhalation.
She is fire before the match is struck.
She speaks to the sleeping man
to infiltrate his dreams.
Words the sleeping man
speaks to her lift and buzz
off to the window.
Her arms are thin as music.
She thirsts for more than touch.
A dress is silent on the floor.
She mouths brown shoulders, presses her tongue.
The room: smoke, a lamp, tea-stained light—
a spinning world, a sapphire ring, a door,
and a locked case that contains
one documented volume
of their skin-in-leather history.
She takes another drag on the cigarette.
Another drink from the wineglass
of the poor wine the widows drink.
Another drag on the cigarette—
and this house of clocks banishes stars.

In Mourning

It is comfortable to be the mourning-ghost (the drowned one), to care for nothing but a petrified sorrow. It is simple to relinquish the will to do anything; to be a stone within a stone within a stone.

The deep end of a cold bath in a house with blinds closed—slivers of natural light and a life-saving measure of patchouli, almond, verbena and tangerine. Deep in trance and desirous of forever's ocean of sleep.

How the woman prays! Her kisses brush his hot forehead. She welcomes him to bed—*When the world comes again we'll awaken.* And it does and they do. Over and over, though no cycle rules her, she rebirths herself. Empties her lungs, rises.

Litany

This morning the house empties its sugar.
This morning something good has gone to rot.
This morning fire catches the pillows under our heads.
This morning the ground quakes with your rising.
This morning the night no longer haunts the air.
This morning the mirror reflects another mirror.
This morning we feed ourselves silence after silence.
This morning we walk into spider webs.
This morning the cup cracks.
This morning: a new sun.
This morning the cat reveals her throat in a yawn.
This morning crooked lines right themselves.
This morning grief sours on our tongues.
This morning is written on a blank sky.
This morning a woman becomes more herself.
This morning there are shards of china under our bare feet.
This morning we weep in our sewing.

Poem to the Madonna

Old mother of sadness,
lie by lie, we feed your sorrow.
Heap hours upon you—each minute a malignancy.

Our insensible prayers:
    one laid upon the other,

        upon the other,
        upon the other,
            with no meaningful
            geometry.

What can we say to you
without poisonous effect?

We know only
that what is was not
until it became.

The bruise-colored garments have fallen away
        to reveal parchment flesh
        hung upon obvious bones,
            a display of wizened genitalia.

    And nearly extinguished now,

        the burning heart.

Barcelona

We arrive with one
bag, and money
hurried out of America.
      All that matters
is the Mediterranean
and the winking ship
      blue upon it.

Blood orange—

communion
to abiding tongues.
The walls are lit
      summer chartreuse.

You close a window.
The song of the street softens.
Your smile obscures,
but there is a beam
      from your eye.

The sun bends the terrace.
Prisms a half-flute of cava.

      And I realize
that nothing—
nothing will come
of this but *love*
to last this day.

Aftermath

She walks into a room
and my heart
splits like a book
broken at its spine
two hands
of pages that beat

How did these words find me
cloistered as I am
in middle worlds?

I fluctuate: rise and rise
until I hunger for oxygen
until no one can see me
no high-powered telescope

I fall and fall; am swallowed
by a hellish mind—

She walks into a room.
My old-woman womb
flutters with illusory children.

She brings me to church.
She brings me to graveyards.

I succumb to all gods
pray for deliverance
and grace falls upon me—
I take a breath
and thank the Almighty I live.

Still, I miss my dead love.
I tell her everything
and she knows how to console me.

As We Are

after the drawing, "Seeking Balance" by Skyler Pham

We began
in a fire of stars.

Life drummed
in our throat

like a god's breath

and we became
as we are.

None can interpret
our transcendent whisperings.

Our salvaged secrets:
more real   in surreality—

O, body- inhabitant,
    we wake and sleep
    a breadth apart,
    lulled by the bloodbeat
    of conjoined hearts.

What life shall we make,
my same-sister?

Your eyes are full
of terrible confessions,

having cried
the nothingness out.

Woman in Prayer

I am penitent;
poured on rail of the pew
somber Mary alit,
red-glassed candles
no smoke, but a hint
of myrrh

The cleaning woman shakes
her mop; blesses herself at the font
and more women
fill in like light
to pray
the stations of the cross

They speak to me and I
decline their invitation—
Their prayers become
my own and I feel the sun exhale

My hanging God, the Christ
that I need to believe in
that I am begging to take
a lifetime's desperation
to deliver me
right my path
crown of thorns
my own heart
brambles and thorns
jag the aorta

what if there were wings?
the blackheart caws
Willfully, I come
for *mercysilence,*
as supplicant—

These women
in devotion, full of grace
could not possibly be
as contrite, as sinful as me.

Because We Love

We mark ourselves with salt.
Tattoo whorls

where blood rushes—
        where blood matters—

What hours do we bring?

Calluses against nipples,
an acid sting.

The sweet grind
of ghost hungers

that ache of our union.
And the ones who hunt us

are blinded
by this, a whiteout sun.

Come, *a Love Poem*

after Brian Baiamonte's "unclouded"

Come to me unburdened.
Come
from the troposphere
of holy contentment.
Free
is how I will take you.
A miniscule promise is all I have.
Is it enough?

I chase the sun
from its peak
to its dissolution. Skin
myself to keep you warm,
love, lover—
boundlessness
contained only by lips
that grasp, release, grasp,
release

I am like these clouds,
open, still, waiting
to be undone by eminent rays.
Between us
there are no inches.
Between us is only breath.
I cannot know—

I am blind today.
I woke up this way.

Touch my brokenness
with your miracle
with your spit and mud,
and I shall be healed.

Thrice

I

Bodies, bodies,
        rungs of bodies—
a gossamer rot   smothers the quiet.

She weeps into a dress
        of pupae
and with her last wicked breath
        draws a midnight cowl

        over you,
succubus
in the mirror.

II

Morning is the pale belly
        of a snake.
Sun-cracks run   to the languid piano.
The senile cat pisses
        on the quilt
        while we silently fuck.

And they tell us *of more bodies.*
        Sobs bully our throats.
Unique fears   squirm in the gut.

        Only sex dispels the hour.

III

Raggedy women coagulate
      at the coffins.

The bald one sneaks
      the wedding rings
from the floured hands of the corpses.
The other slips   venom
      into Styrofoam cups,
from which we all
      drink.

Body in Place

I could explain my body—

a construct of the carcasses
of horses burned in a locked barn—

I could explain it to you,
my Griever and Malcontent.

I could explain my lips—white
china, black tea. The door
in my chest opens and light
floods in as I sweep the dead
flies across the threshold.

My naked thighs bob in a coral sea.
My arms, eviscerated, pull from their roots.
My feet have flown off; migrated
to winter across the Gulf of Mexico.

My tongue, heart and cunt
have been carved out. I have
this swath of skin, a calamity
of bones and half-used eyes—

The decision has been made
to take you as a lover.
You must divine
a new paradigm to enter
      and know me.

Body

after Myriam Jégat's "Dingle"

I am a million bodies
laid upon each other
a million bodies
in a mass grave
ocean carried me
here as I broke
from the mountain
the rain
chisels my limbs
from limbs we are
disparate parts
the ocean birthed
the sky, the sky
departed and I lay
here treacherous
disguised as rock
my breath shallow
overcome by waves
no one can hear
the single word
I speak: despair.

Barghest

The growl is deafening; splits a cerulean thunderhead. What mythical wonder woke you?

Sleep executed by firing squad. (Oh, the marksman without a bullet cries and the woman trained on his finger languishes).

He who has blood on his temple will never raise the stone in his fist.

We keep the sins we commit. What is a secret if no one cares to know?

Hunger, hunger from the day you were terribly born. (This is why she hates you). There is no milk for children made of glass.

That which is left behind is all for you. The curse is that you cannot touch it. Remember what came to you through death will go through you like water. Still, the dead keep giving.

Wind shoves its tongue down your throat. A brass bird revels in rain. Someone runs into traffic with an inverted umbrella, dances, and shakes loose coins from her belly.

Hunger, again, for dog meat, good enough to eat, so, why not eat it? Filaments of lightning sear your morning-eye then burn out.

Phones ring with too much treble. Every time it is her–*I want you back*. The house shakes. Sleep explodes like a plane crashing to the ground.

It was wrong of me to take a swig of vodka at the funeral. I did not want it, or its meaning. The priest held it against me. I never confessed.

I pity the most unusual things. And there was no charm in this creature: dwindling fur, black, broken teeth, ember-eyes and skin thin as a frog's. Nauseating.

Why did it come here? Was it for souls? I thought to feed it bloody meat hung on a wooden stick, but it took what it came for.

The sun rises and we hunger. The sun sets and we hunger. It is the only hunger that matters.

For the Electrocuted Owl

We bend to blacktop to better see,
to eye the majestic—
And quivering with gravity
succumb to the helpless
state we must suffer
when attacked by forces
unnamed and unknown
compelling us to stay rooted,
frozen, and so inescapably speak:

> *O glorious;*
> *splayed in moon-devotion;*
> *night descends on silent wings;*
> *cream-belly angel with black*
> *pearl eyes; o wind blade;*
> *this dew is blood; this killing fire*
> *whistles in bone; you*
> *lightless dead lie in sick streams,*
> *utterly gone.*

Stasis

   after "Woodpecker" by Anne Elezabeth Pluto

The woodpecker's heart
still as bedrock
blood absent
not a drop on concrete (fingers
of leaves, laced
black metal)

What exists in stasis
exists
like a star exists
out of reach;
close as bone

light lifts
from a seabed
dust in a room stirs
when a woman stirs
to turn her body
from the sleeping lover

his back, a light sheen
of fragrant oil, blue
aura of morning sleep

a blind man innately knows
black wing tips
the deaf man innately knows
the death-song

of each living thing
as they exit
our presence

fall away winter,
become unknowable

ice
no longer penetrates
the eye
when fire
comes to the city

the woman leaves
her lover's bed
and leaves the man
she loves for he
who makes her volcanic

blood, snow, and mud
unburdened air
vibrant green shoots
entwine carcasses
all over the planet

"Be gone, rust, be gone!"
the woodpecker spoke its trill

such is the mortification of all flesh
and we, too, are mortified
as one

Meditation on "Intimations of Winter II"

after the photograph, "Intimations of Winter II" by Zeralda La Grange

There is a harmony
        in the commingling
of light

        and dark—ghost patterns
formed on
        snow-sodden

ground.   All in stasis, here,
        broken glints

hang mid-air
        and still
                the cypress rots.

How do we speak
        the dead-etchings
                of grass?

This artifice,
        in the infinitesimal,

has lost from view
                the on/off pulse

        of blue-black wings.

The only hint
        of their affect

was held in the breath
                of the artist

and not entrapped
in the gloss

of this picture.

Convergence

after the photograph "Burdened Sky" by Zeralda La Grange

We wait   for the landscape
    to split
from these two dimensions.

The lens
    is half-asleep
or engaged
        in meditation.

We hope
    that a stray,
a cur,
will jog
    across the grave
limestone, or wish

    for dead
    leaves
to rise
    mythically.

Ghost wheels   ghost-whistle.
    The whole scene
    distills
to black,
    to white— unleashing
the indomitable
        core.

    Railway lines
        converge.
The sky becomes
        burdened
with a broken
    Jesus—
        one rusted spike   through his palm.

Ink on a Mirror

after the photograph "Stark Lines" by Zeralda La Grange

The shooter
        must have
leaned in,

before clenching
        her trigger finger.

Immaculate power
    to still
life more deeply,
           exercised.

In this stand,

      trees
      are lank,

piebald horses sleeping.

Black ink
     spills
onto a mirror.

The dull knife
          scrapes
     at light.

How it Comes

Sometimes it comes in a sleep
in which you dream of the blackest horses.

It comes riding on the strong back of the animal,
or is tangled in its mane. Often, it is

itself the glowing coal of an eye,
which burns through you.

Sometimes it comes from the air,
rising from the strangeness of a threatening sky.

Wind exhales it into your ear,
or it seeps through the ground

like the fresh spring;
then it chills us—

It comes in the body of nature, or not.
It is not always a mystery.

It may come to you in the memory
of a city; perhaps San Francisco

or New Orleans or Tucson.
Or in the recollection

of the first and last kiss
of someone you loved, or did not.

Today it came to me
as a bird; its wingbeat

light as a whisper, pecking
fruit in a verdant heart.

A Rain Like No Other

after John Slaughter's "RAIN / MARFA / TEXAS"

The land is suddenly lost.
So much to bear.
Red is heavy.
It lightens only
as God's hands
stroke and smite.
The electric eye captures
the voluminous image.
Technologic whisper
with authority   to stop
the whole world.

Heaven in sheer descent.
A rain like no other.

Such vividness wakes worlds
from stone sleep.
Resonant coral—a new
energy commands:

Reel your act of vengeance;
just be.

Do not take another step
until you have breathed
a full hour
with eyes set upon me

Of the Gone Woman

Black and white,
    you are vagrant
        in a still picture,

    scarred daughter
    of a bitter moon.

You cursed me to live
among snakes,
    among stars.

You bequeathed falsities
and humiliations—

But I have unremembered
your myths
    and pray to dispel

        their bad magic.

I have nothing left
with which to create
    an effigy —

Mother,
you skimmed your finger
along my bone
and left a print
    inside.

Phoenix

for Kelly

She merely dreamt of fire and flames materialized in her room. Even shadow burned and no water flowed from her mouth. No tears fell from her seared eyes. Her lungs, curling pages, black—all was blackened, yes. All that she had ever been was cinder-blown, and a palpable fate overwhelmed her. What remained, the incorruptible self, rose to the ceiling. The ceiling opened. She that she was rose to the sky. The sky opened. She, her self, became storm, the gaseous star, the sun, beams of other moons. There was no death in her and she embodied many things: lava on a bleak terrain; a flooded river once cracked dry, and wood rooted in earth. She became earth, too, and succumbed to worms. She became hollow. She became full. No longer the mounted wife or bone-bearer, no longer a woman weeping bitter shards of mourning. Huntress, seductress, heathen and whore made new in body, new in word.

What Came After

I had been craving you and felt
the earth quiver for an instant
and thought of your feet
bare on rocks at the coast
of the island and we engaged
our thoughts in those horrific
seconds to meet in the only
way the gods would allow
through the ether our thoughts
locked in stony-motion.
We are bound to our villages.
We are bound to the rubble
that is our beds. And I sprang
to attention when the sun broke
like the yolk of a duck's egg.
The sun looms so brightly; bloody and real.
We named ourselves after mountains
but forgot what shifted beneath us.
Why does the earth hate me so,
to take you from me?
The sea took me into its mouth
and spit me out onto broken wood.
I floated with corpses. My history
unraveled all at once. I became no one.

Eiffel Tower, a Recollection of Paris, 1986

It punctuates the sky
and reminds me
of what I missed

of the city those three days
in a Frenchman's apartment
that did not overlook the Seine

or the tower itself, but bricks,
crumbling and raining red
dust on feral streets of Paris.

I sought in open windows
something of myself
and something of the man

with whom I did not share
a language but an ineffable
knowledge. This small,

plastic replica, a token,
a souvenir someone laid
upon a shelf, is a terror.

I fear the heights
to which it would take me
and the fall that would kill me

if you ever let me go. I never
visited the spire; never put
my tongue on cold iron,

or ran my fingers
on braided metal fashioned
as an exaltation of man.

For three days I lived
in the bed of a stranger
whose ferocity of body

upon body consumed me
amidst soft chords rising—
like the music of the street.

Refuge

The flutist
whispers *labia*
between breaths

a dragonfly zips on air

no darker doorways
no storm
to carry off the house—

Please, tonight, hold me
with the remembrance of light.

Secrets Alluded to but Never Told

    i.   Sunset
               is the fringe of the world.
               (Nothing exists beyond it).
    ii.   Lions sprawl in cusps   of clouds. The sky
    iii.   is edged in bird-smoke.
    iv.   When the world
               is doused
               in blue *stormlight,*
               wild mares break
               from their herds.

Seeing Through

Take me deeply, other.
I am frantic with life—

I see you through the doorway
as you enter sunlight.

You expand into light,
touching the edge of the forest.

Your shape embosses
the far line of the horizon.

I would follow you to places
with forgotten names.

I have followed you here
to the precipice of being.

You are all to me.

Without you I would become
blood-thin, full of grief—

laden with omens
of one remembered kiss.

I see you at the crossing
as shadow embraces you.

Shadow rims your hazy visage;
shadow like moss or coal-smoke.

Take me deeply, other.
I am frantic with life.

Sky Burial

Leave me
on open land
until bonesong
goes unheard
and all putrefaction
resolves.

Let me cultivate
the growth
of all that is visible
and invisible—
be the giver
of alms to the birds.

My secret name
is *Carrion*.

Dead
or living come,
come to commune.
Let us go with eyes open
into ineffable light.

The Artist and His Model

Moon rooted in wood.
Woman rooted in shadow.
Shadow drapes her nude figure.
The light is as he wants.
Her hands spread on her belly.
Her hands network to her spine.
She arches her back.
Belly to the moon
which wanes in the wood.
Every muscle aches
for the silent cue
to release supine.
Her thoughts unravel.
She gives one
to the maestro
with sable brushes.
He swipes her knee
with cadmium
in his excitement.
Close as breath. Close enough
to hear the tinny heartbeat
tick away in his chest.
Or is it a wheeze?
He mixes a cerulean eye.
A small hammer
beats behind her knee.
He permits her
to slump into pillows.
A brushstroke grows wild.
Something bubbles
in her tummy. The child
in a blood balloon.
The baby's kick
is a fresh flute of cava.
He tells her to breathe,
hold out her palm.
In it, he places a nectarine.

What We Carry

broken bottles
and rusted things

gasoline-soaked rags
a knife wet with blood

the tail feather
of a rooster

sewing needles
a burnt match

a fistful of sins

the stain of roses
a storm of horses

letters from the dead

all in solemnity
all in solemnity

embodied in the sunken hull—
itself, an ocean

The Embalmer's Wife

You've never revealed
your dreams but I guess

the dreamscape:
faces like cold candles,

water-stone eyes,
sewn mouths—viscera.

*She was a weaver who imparted
wisdom to her daughters.*

She was devout.

Cherish my breast
and the music

of our breathing.
Heartbeat-cadences lilt

in the hours we share.
I cling to you gratefully.

How you touch me with need,
surrender to life.

All This Remembering

I dreamed again
of the bloody foal
born in winter.
Night
after night, her dying—

It is a dark awakening; wind
skitters across the lake.
The woods are whispering muses.

I am afraid to go
where memory takes me.

*My only child
stares me down
with hatred
while a tube is snaked
down her throat. A black
foaming slick of pill
fragments
drains out of her mouth—*

I am afraid to go
beyond what is now,
and now and now.

Forgetting will not be the end.

The wind speaks wolf
as I drag on a cigarette,
contemplating an ember's
becoming into ash.

The trees distill
to charcoal lines
on a black page.

The Hand You Hold

is a river stone:
      supple,
            untouched by salt.

And months before,
      before this mean sickness,
            this same hand felt
    like a summer
        of no rain.

Now he is flaccid
      and cold, waking
           only to whisper

        nightmares,

    willfully mislead
by their gift of fear—

These hands hewed wood,
turned wrenches

        until they could no longer
           hold anything

but another hand
      in a dark room
           while both bodies
            contemplate the nature

                of impermanence.

The Raw Heart

saturated/blistered
hard and foul
can keep us living
though for not an eternity
self-solace
a lace of fat
discordant beats
fan the veins
a simple resolution
to a complex problem
dig deep
in the dirt, the dirge
of bloodsong murmurs

stillness to absolution

The Word Does Not Come

I am bare; always yearning.
No path leads from this want.

I've spread myself open,
made a nest of my heart.

I have torn out pages
wishing to forget.

I have gone into the poem
and taken

poetry inside me,
but the word does not come.

What is it of me that kills?

I am dropping deeper,
        deeper into the hush—

Thunder found me
and perpetual rain fell upon me.
You enter. Forbidden,
forbidden touch which excites me so—
How did I come to you,
beloved, so undone and unabashed?
Our fingers make alphabets
on each other's skin
and we guess the words we make.
Mine: forget. Yours: remember.
I have forgotten all of my vulnerabilities.
I have forgotten my vow or relinquished it,
to this higher love, on the altar of your body.
Our movements are slow; our eyes keep pace.
Each pulse a kiss, each kiss quickens the blood's beating.
I knew if I began to write, I would write a love poem to you.
A poem to express this fragile sin
that engenders in me encompassing horror, and joy—

When Bones Have Forgotten

When bones have forgotten
the sun and all
they remember is ache;
or one road
in a cold wood
the wolf howl
and fevers
that never broke—
When hands have forgotten
the feel of salt sea
ramifications of love
or the silenced and silent
in times of war—
When eyes unremember
the grimace of a child
before the hacking begins;
or the recipe for poison
ink washed by tears—
When the throat remembers
whiskey-flames
that spark the fool's
retort
and shackles
that do not break;
(rusted, crisp
as footfall on frost).
This metal,
strung with barbs,
strangles voice—
Now,
remember
money
feeds the wrong
and the wronged—
sometimes.
And World says,
"The door is sealed.
Stay behind it."

A Tale

after Brian Baiamonte's "Grandma used to take me here"

My brother fled to another Earth.

Perhaps he followed
the trail of birds
left on the path—

The old one lives in the wood
beyond the collapsed well.
Her face is a web of veins.
Her hands:
severed crow's wings.

I am her captive. For three days,
she oils my skin; kneads
muscles with her knuckles.
All the while
she sharpens blades.

But, I've grown too close
to womanhood to butcher.

Instead, she blinds me.
Plucks out my eyes and feeds
them to her cur for a trick—

She makes a bed for us
of pelts and pillows filled
with swans' down.

This night, the witch in me
unravels; and by morning—
I demolish her
with a kiss.

A Story

A wolf went blind, died and was fed on by scavengers. The gristle that remained decayed and maggots swirled. On a cold morning, after days of rain, these wolf bones crack under the footfall of a man. The man carries a shotgun and a flask as he walks in the wood. He is thin and holds one fractured belief. I will not tell you what it is. He has a sweet side, or so they say, but that is not a necessary detail in the story. This man woke this morning with an erection that his wife would not satisfy. The man is looking for something to kill and a cure for his erection. The day heats up. Crows caw his coming into the sky. The man takes a swig from the flask and rubs his wet nose with a camouflage glove. The animals smell him and stay hidden. The man picks up a sheer bone from the carcass of the wolf and sniffs it. He is all of fifty-eight and is no longer employable. The man puts the bone in the chest-pocket of his denim overalls. The man remembers something and forgets it almost as quickly. Then, he remembers his mother's saying that "It must not be important." But it was. Why are we concerned with this man? He is not the story. The story is of starving wolves, bones, rotting viscera, the callous vultures that circle a small clearing in a wood after days and days of rain. This story is of the matter we are made of, return to; our shared transformation.

Across the Universe

The times my mind
betrayed me I cannot
say, day to day
If I rise I am saved
If I lie in bed without light
I am saved
blinds shut /sunny day
take a bath eat
something
      I am saved
pray
desire *to be right*
(and righteousness is not
what you think)
do not speak harm to yourself
      or others
do not exhibit symptoms
and they will not take you
thank you *breathe* thank
you *breathe* O, Enemy,
thank you for your purpose
you make my will a rod
      through me
Open, or in a box?
Sometimes small, yes.
Beloved dead & living
voices surround me
a word/a handwritten note
subatomic change
      of being
even spittle spurs
butterfly
to typhoon
      to newborn star

End Note

She slips out, disguising herself as a shadow. Moving slow as shadow: a lengthening mark against decreasing light.

Beyond the open field, where the patients do calisthenics each morning, there is a hedgerow, and beyond that a gate. To the field before someone notices. Beyond the field to the gate before they know. She slips into a green abyss.

Her bare feet skim the mud. She drips dark mud as each foot rises. A decrepit thought enters her mind. She turns back, just momentarily, to see the brick-bone building almost in ruin. She cries seed after seed into slim furrows her toes created.

She must punch in a code to enter or exit. She does not know if she is entering or exiting. She climbs the gate. Someone shouts. She climbs down the gate. She runs. She runs until it is night. The North Star is obscured and she wouldn't know it anyway. She wishes for a river to follow a down-flow. She knows people in the South. But, perhaps, they don't love her anymore?

All of her imaginings, innumerable, sorrowful, soul-stealing sinister, become sheer, so that she can almost see through them (but unfortunately cannot).

It begins to rain. For every raindrop a black feather falls. Blackbird-eyes are upon her. She hunches from heaviness of the scattered wings; swallows a mouthful of naked moon.

Her days and nights culminate into the fullest sun. She murmurs: Is it or is it not, and why?

Somehow, impossibly, the world softens around her. Her idea of God softens, too. The one and only voice she possesses constellates with discorporate multitudes in harmonic undulations.

Holy holy holy

Acknowledgments

The author would like to acknowledge the editors and publishers of the literary journals in which the following poems first appeared, and gratefully, the many individuals in the Acadiana writing community with whom she shared writing time over the course of years.

A Clean, Well-Lighted Place: "How It Comes," "Meditation on 'Intimation of Winter II'"
blue five notebook: "Seeing Through," "Seek the Holy Dark"
Degrees of Separation: "A Rain Like No Other," "A Tale," "Body," "Come, a Love Poem"
Louisiana Literature: "Convergence," "Ink on a Mirror"
MadHat Annual: "The lover who does not come until morning," "Litany," "Thrice," "Body In Place," "Thunder found me."
Melusine, or Woman in the 21st Century: "The Embalmer's Wife"
Sunrise from Blue Thunder: An Anthology: "What Came After"
Unlikely Stories: "All This Remembering," "Because We Love," "Dream of Sudden Water," "Of the Gone Woman," "Poem to the Madonna," "Secrets Alluded to but Never Told," "The Word Does Not Come"
Vision/Verse 2009-2013: An Anthology of Poetry: "As We Are"
Yellow Flag Press: "As We Are"

Great thanks are expressed to Bessie Senette for assistance in the acquisition of rights to use the cover art, "Birds if Time" by Agnieszka Nowinska.

Dedicated to the women in my life. Most especially, Bessie Senette, who, with seriousness and love, pointed a finger at me and said, "You need to write another damn book."

About the Author

Photo Credit: Tammie Simon

Clare L. Martin's debut collection of poetry, *Eating the Heart First*, was published in 2012 by Press 53. Martin's poetry has appeared in *Avatar Review, Blue Fifth Review, Thrush Poetry Journal, Melusine, Poets and Artists,* and *Louisiana Literature,* among others. She has been nominated for a Pushcart Prize, Dzanc Books' *Best of the Web, Best New Poets,* and Sundress Publication's *Best of the Net.* Martin is Founding Publisher and Editor of *MockingHeart Review.* She is a lifelong resident of Louisiana.

The Louisiana Series
of Cajun and Creole Poetry

La Série de Louisiane
de Poésie des Acadiens et Créoles

Series Editor: J. Bruce Fuller

The Louisiana Series of Cajun and Creole Poetry was founded to highlight work done by exceptional poets of Franco-American descent. Yellow Flag Press is proud to publish new work by poets of Cajun, Creole, or French heritage, writing in French, Cajun French, English, or works in translation.

Titles in the Series

if you abandon me, comment je vas faire: An Amédé Ardoin Songbook
Darrell Bourque

Elliptic
Jack B. Bedell

Seek the Holy Dark
Clare L. Martin